LUCIA FÖRTHMANN

Baby Shoes to Crochet

FASHIONABLE STYLES FOR LITTLE FEET

Search Press

First published in Great Britain 2016 by
Search Press Limited
Wellwood, North Farm Road
Tunbridge Wells, Kent TN2 3DR

© Edition Michael Fischer GmbH, 2015

This translation of BABYSCHÜHCHEN TICK first published in
Germany by Edition Michael Fischer GmbH in 2015 is published by
arrangement with Silke Bruenink Agency, Munich, Germany.

English Translation by Burravoe Translation Services

Cover design: Tim Anadere
Editor: Anna Zwicklbauer
Proofreading: Ute Wielandt
Layout and typesetting: Silvia Keller
Photos: Ziska Thalhammer, Munich
Illustrations: Susanne Bochem, Mainz

ISBN: 978-1-78221-357-4
ebook: 978-1-78126-401-0

If you have difficulty in obtaining any of the materials and equipment
mentioned in this book, then please visit the Search Press website
for details of suppliers: www.searchpress.com

Printed in China

ACKNOWLEDGEMENTS

My deepest thanks go to my wonderful family, and in particular to my husband, who has always supported me, especially on days that were unbelievably busy. Thank you so much for your patience with my chaotic streak, and your tolerance of the balls of yarn that sometimes found their way all around the house!

A big kiss for my three enchanting children who, whenever needed, were able to come up with new crochet ideas for me.

Thank you to all of my friends, who sent me light from afar that gave me strength. You are always in my heart.

Many thanks to Heidi of Heidi's Strickbar. I can always find the perfect yarn for my new projects in your small but beautifully appointed 'yarn paradise'.

Huge thanks to Charlotte May, Lena Steghöfer and Anna Zwicklbauer, and to the entire team at Edition Michael Fischer, for their active support and the wonderful creation of this book.

Thanks also to the loyal readers of my blog and fans of my crocheted work.

CONTENTS

FOR LITTLE LADIES

WILD THING!

SPORTY & CHEEKY

SUMMER, SUN & SANDALS

INTRODUCTION

A baby is on the way! Pregnancy is a time of growth, preparation and anticipation. With a first baby in particular, a mum-to-be often still has far too much time to think, spending hours considering the new arrival's wardrobe, and by the end of the pregnancy she may find herself becoming rather impatient with the whole business.

That's certainly how I felt in all three of my pregnancies. So what could be more enjoyable than spending hours looking around a yarn shop, and then later settling back in a chair to crochet a whole range of tiny shoes and booties in every possible colour, variation and size for the baby?

I would like this book to give you the motivation and encouragement to create your own versions for your little one. Then, after the birth, you can put on a really special performance as you appear in matching footwear, whether elegant, sporty or casual. And if you can't yet crochet – well, then you have nine months to learn before you find the baby taking up all of your time. Make the most of it!

And if you're not pregnant? Well, then it makes even more sense to take up your crochet hook and make a lovely little gift for a friend who is! Or perhaps two or three? But a word of warning: you could find yourself becoming addicted.

Happy crocheting,

Lucia Förthmann

CROCHET BASICS

HOW DO I START?

Depending on the instructions, you start either with a row of chain stitches or a magic ring.

ROW OF CHAIN STITCHES

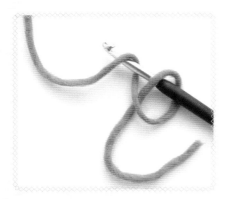

1. Shape the end of the yarn into a loop. Insert the hook through the loop.

2. Yarn over hook and draw through the loop.

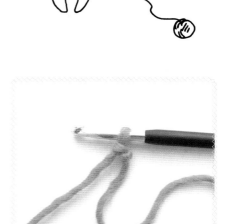

3. Pull the end of the yarn to tighten the loop. You have made a slip knot.

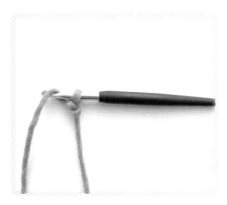

4. Move the hook under the yarn, yarn over hook and pull through the loop on the hook. You have now crocheted a chain stitch (ch).

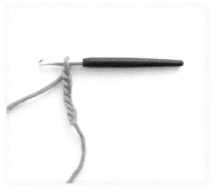

5. Repeat this process by the number of chain stitches required for the pattern. This is what a row of chain stitches looks like.

6. To continue crocheting in rows, insert the hook through the second chain stitch from the hook. For a half double (half treble) crochet stitch, insert the hook in the third chain, and for double crochet (treble) in the fourth chain from the hook.

THE MAGIC RING

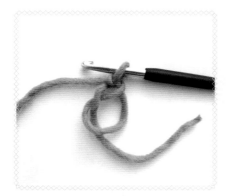

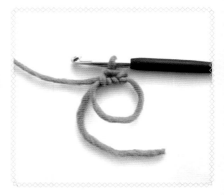

1. For a magic ring, make the yarn into a loop as for the row of chain stitches, and draw the yarn tail through. However, rather than tightening the loop, crochet a chain stitch.

2. Insert the hook into the ring, yarn over hook and draw through the ring. You will crochet around the yarn tail. You now have two loops on the hook.

3. Yarn over hook and draw through both of the loops on the hook. You have made your first single crochet (sc; double crochet, dc)!

4. Crochet five more single crochet (double crochet) stitches into the ring in the same way.

5. Pull the yarn tail tight to close the hole in the centre.

6. Insert the hook into the first stitch, yarn over hook and draw through the loop on the hook. You have now crocheted a slip stitch (sl st)!

TIP

If you crochet a magic ring of double crochet (treble), start the first round with three ch for the first double crochet (treble). Finish the round with one sl st into the third ch of the first double crochet (treble).

7. The magic ring is now complete.

You killed four birds with one stone when you learnt how to make a magic ring. You can now crochet chain stitches, single crochet (double crochet), slip stitches and a magic ring. They are all described again here for when you want to refer back to them later on:

SLIP STITCH (SL ST)

1. Insert the hook into the stitch.

2. Yarn over hook and draw through the stitch and the loop on the hook.

SINGLE CROCHET (SC; UK DOUBLE CROCHET, DC)

1. Insert the hook in the stitch, yarn over hook and draw through stitch. You will now have two loops on the hook.

2. Yarn over hook again, and draw through both loops.

DOUBLE CROCHET (DC; UK TREBLE, TR)

1. Yarn over hook once. This is also known as a yarn over, or 'YO'.

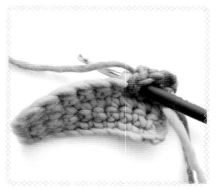

2. Now insert the hook into the stitch, yarn over hook and draw through the stitch.

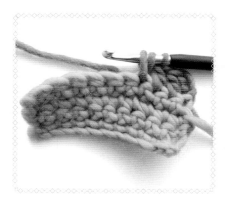

3. You will now have three loops on the hook.

4. Yarn over hook and draw through the first two loops on the hook. Two loops will remain on the hook.

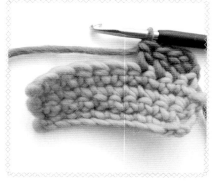

5. Yarn over hook one last time, then draw through the two remaining loops to complete the stitch.

HALF DOUBLE CROCHET (HDC; UK HALF TREBLE, HTR)

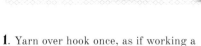

1. Yarn over hook once, as if working a double crochet (treble).

2. Insert the hook into the stitch, yarn over hook and draw through stitch. You will have three loops on the hook. Yarn over hook once more, and draw through all through three loops on the hook.

3. You have completed a half double crochet (half treble).

JOINING NEW YARN

1. Insert the hook into the stitch, new yarn over hook and draw through stitch.

2. Yarn over hook again, and draw through the loop on the hook.

TREBLE CROCHET (TR; UK DOUBLE TREBLE, DTR)

1. Yarn over hook twice.

2. Insert the hook into the stitch, yarn over hook and draw through stitch. You will have four loops on the hook.

3. Yarn over hook and draw through the first two loops on the hook. You will now have three loops on the hook.

4. Yarn over hook again, and draw through the first two loops. You will now have two loops left on the hook.

5. Yarn over hook one last time, then draw through the last two loops on the hook.

CHANGING COLOURS

1. Work most of the last stitch of a row in the existing colour.

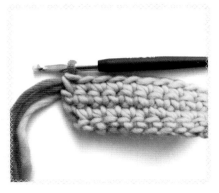

2. Finish the last part of the stitch in the new colour.

INCREASING (INC)

Work two stitches in one stitch of the previous row or round. This increases the number of stitches by one.

DECREASING (DEC)

To decrease, work two stitches together. This reduces the number of stitches by one. The method of decreasing may differ depending on the kind of stitch being used.

FOR SINGLE CROCHET (UK DOUBLE CROCHET):

1. Insert the hook into the first stitch, yarn over hook and draw through the stitch. Insert the hook into the second stitch, yarn over hook and draw through the stitch. You will have three loops on the hook.

2. Yarn over hook and draw through all three loops to complete the decrease.

FOR HALF DOUBLE CROCHET (UK HALF TREBLE):

Yarn over hook, insert into the first stitch, yarn over hook and draw through stitch. Yarn over hook again, insert hook into second stitch, yarn over hook and draw through the stitch. You will now have five loops on the hook. Yarn over hook again, and draw through all five loops on the hook to complete the decrease.

FOR DOUBLE CROCHET (TREBLE):

1. Yarn over hook, insert into the first stitch, yarn over hook and draw through stitch.

2. Yarn over hook, insert into the second stitch, yarn over hook and draw through stitch. You will now have five loops on the hook.

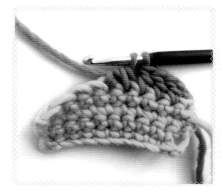

3. Yarn over hook and draw through the first four loops on the hook so that two loops remain.

4. Yarn over hook one last time, then draw through the remaining two loops to complete the decrease.

FRONT POST DOUBLE CROCHET (TREBLE)

1. Yarn over hook once. Do not insert the hook into the actual stitch but a little lower, from the front and to the right of the stem (post) of the stitch. Move the hook around the back of the stem so it comes back out to the front, to the left of the stem (post).

2. Yarn over hook, and draw it all the way around the stem (post) and out.

3. Finish the double crochet (treble) stitch as usual.

BACK POST DOUBLE CROCHET (TREBLE)

1. Yarn over hook once. Do not insert the hook in the actual stitch, but a little lower, from the back and to the right of the stem (post) of the stitch.

2. Move the hook around the front of the stem (post), and insert it from the front and to the left of the stem (post) so it comes out at the back again. Yarn over hook, and draw it all the way around the stem (post) and out.

3. Finish the double crochet (treble) stitch as usual.

POST STITCHES FROM THE BACK

1. Post stitches worked from the back are very good for creating steps and edges within a crocheted item. Do not insert the hook in the actual stitch, but from the back and to the right of it.

2. Move the hook around the front of the stem (post), and insert it from the front and to the left of the stitch to the back.

3. Yarn over hook, then draw it all the way around the stitch and out. Finish the stitch as usual.

WORKING STITCHES INTO THE PREVIOUS ROW

1. This is exactly what it says: the stitches are worked into the same stitches in the previous row or round.

2. This is what it looks like. It is also called a long single crochet (double) stitch, or spike stitch.

3. The instructions in your pattern will tell you if you have to work a stitch lower than in the previous round. Take care not to work the stitch too tightly so that you don't end up pulling the area out of shape.

STITCHES WORKED FROM THE BACK

Insert the hook into the back loop only of the two loops at the top of the stitch. Work the required stitch as usual.

WORKING INTO THE BACK LOOP OF THE STITCH

Insert the hook into the back loop only of the two loops at the top of the stitch. Work the required stitch as usual.

WORKING INTO THE FRONT LOOP OF THE STITCH

Insert the hook into the front loop only of the two loops at the top of the stitch. Work the required stitch as usual.

WHIPSTITCH

Sew this stitch by hand to join two edges together. Insert the needle at the back and out through the front of an edge, then insert it at a slight angle through the front and out through the back of the opposite edge. Now move the needle sideways from the back and out through the front of the first edge, and repeat this step as often as necessary.

TULIP STITCH (T ST)

Yarn over hook once, then insert the hook into the stitch and draw the yarn through. You will now have three loops on the hook. Repeat twice more. You will have seven loops on the hook. Yarn over hook, then draw through all seven loops to complete the stitch.

MATTRESS STITCH

This stitch is used to sew two pieces of work together without a visible seam.

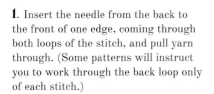

1. Insert the needle from the back to the front of one edge, coming through both loops of the stitch, and pull yarn through. (Some patterns will instruct you to work through the back loop only of each stitch.)

2. Insert the needle through the next stitch from front to back, then from the back to the front of the stitch on the opposite edge and pull yarn through.

3. Then insert the needle through the next stitch from front to back, move it across to the other edge and insert the needle from back to front of the stitch on the opposite edge again, pulling the yarn through. Repeat these steps until you reach the end, then pull the yarn quite taut so that it 'disappears' and fuses the two edges together. Fasten off yarn and weave in the loose end.

USEFUL NOTES

Secure and cut yarn
To secure the yarn at the end of a piece of work and prevent it from being cut off, make two chain stitches. Then cut the yarn about 6in (15cm) along, thread it through the last chain stitch and tighten.

Neatening
Sew in any loose ends with an embroidery or tapestry needle to neaten them. Carefully weave the yarn through the stitches of the previous row or round, ideally so they cannot be seen.

How do I work a round?
At the end of a round, work a slip stitch into the first stitch of the round to close it. Work one chain stitch (turning chain) and continue without turning. If the first stitch in the round is a double crochet (treble) work three chain stitches instead, and two chain stitches for a half double crochet (half treble) to achieve the same stitch height.

How do I work a spiral round?
Continue working at the end of the round without working a slip stitch. As it is then not possible to see where the round begins, it is a good idea to insert a stitch marker through the first stitch in the round. This eliminates the need for tedious counting.

How do I work a row?
Work a turning chain at the end of the row, then turn the work. Sometimes the instructions will tell you to work an additional slip stitch into the first stitch of the round or row. If the first stitch in the row is a double crochet (treble), then work three chain stitches instead, and two chain stitches instead of a half double crochet (half treble) to achieve the same stitch height.

Alternative yarn
If you cannot source the yarns stated in the patterns, you can use a yarn of a similar weight and yardage to make the shoes and boots in this book.

What is gauge (tension)?

Everybody has their own unique way of crocheting. Some people's work is quite loose, while other people crochet quite tightly, and that is why it is important to check the gauge (or tension). Patterns usually indicate how many rows and stitches will be in a piece measuring 4 x 4in (10 x 10cm).

Depending on your personal way of crocheting, you might have to use a smaller or larger hook, or work more tightly or loosely, to get the right results. If, for instance, you don't have enough stitches in the sample piece, you will either have to crochet more tightly or use a smaller hook. If you have too many stitches, do the opposite; crochet more loosely or use a larger hook. Bear in mind that it is easier to adjust your gauge (tension) by changing your hook size than by crocheting more tightly or loosely.

In my instructions, I sometimes also provide the length and width of the area made up by 10 rows of 10 stitches. This can result in a more precise gauge (tension).

Fit

If a crocheted bootie slips off your baby's foot, use an embroidery needle and a few running stitches to sew in a piece of elastic to the back of the shoe opening. Note that the elastic should be pulled taut while you sew it on to make the shoe opening a little narrower.

ABBREVIATIONS

As many of the steps are repeated in the instructions, we use abbreviations:

bp dc	back post double crochet (UK treble, tr)
bp st	back post stitch
ch	chain
col	colour
dc	double crochet (UK treble, tr)
dec	decrease
fp st	front post stitch
fp dc	front post double crochet (UK treble, tr)
hdc	half double crochet (UK half treble, htr)
inc	increase
l	length
rd	round
rep	repeat
sc	single crochet (UK double crochet, dc)
sl st	slip stitch
st	stitch
t st	tulip stitch
tr	treble crochet (UK double treble, dtr)
tog	together
YO	yarn over
WS	wrong side

NOTE

Babies can easily swallow small items, so sew over any small pieces two or three times to secure them, and carefully neaten the threads.

INSTRUCTIONS FOR SOLES

The basic instructions and the individual crochet instructions for the booties are given in three sizes:

Size 1: 0–3 months (length of shoe sole approx. 4in (10cm))
Size 2: 3–6 months (length of shoe sole approx. 4¼in (11cm))
Size 3: 6–9 months (length of shoe sole approx. 4¾in (12cm))

The information for babies aged 0–3 months is given first, for babies from 3 months it is between the forward slashes, and the figures for babies from 6 months of age are last: 0–3 months/3–6 months/6–9 months. If only one figure is given, it applies to all the sizes.

The soles are all worked in rounds. Work 1 ch at the beginning of the round, and finish the round with 1 sl st into the first st of the round. Do not turn.

Rd 1: Work 13/15/16 ch in your chosen colour. Work 1 sc (dc)/1 hdc (htr)/1 hdc (htr) into the 2nd ch from the hook, then 1 sc (dc)/1 hdc (htr)/1 hdc (htr) into the next 10/12/13 ch, 3 sc (dc)/3 hdc (htr)/3 hdc (htr) into the last ch. Do not turn work, but continue crocheting on the other side of the length of chains: 10 sc (dc)/12 hdc (htr)/13 hdc (htr), 2 sc (dc)/2 hdc (htr)/2 hdc (htr) into the last st (the st you worked the first st into at the beginning) (26/30/32 sts).

Rd 2: Inc 1 st, 10/12/13 sc (dc), inc 1 st 3 times, 10/12/13 sc (dc), inc 1 st twice (32/36/38 sts).

Rd 3: 6/8/8 sc (dc), 3/3/4 hdc (htr), 3 dc (tr), 2 dc (tr) into 1 st 6 times, 3 dc (tr), 3/3/4 hdc (htr), 6/8/8 sc (dc), inc 1 st twice (40/44/46 sts).

Rd 4: Inc 1 st, 5/7/7 sc (dc), 3/3/4 hdc (htr), 6 dc (tr), 2 dc (tr) into 1 st 6 times, 6 dc (tr), 3/3/4 hdc (htr), 6/8/8 sc (dc) inc 1 st 4 times (51/55/57 sts).

Rd 5: 1 st into each st of the previous rd (51/55/57 sts).

Either secure the yarn or continue working in the required colour, according to the pattern.

TIP

With a little practice, it won't take you long to crochet a sole. Crochet one to check the gauge (tension), and compare the length with the information provided above. If you are making booties for a 'preemie', use a smaller hook or work a little more tightly. By the same token, use a larger hook or work a little more loosely to make the booties in the third size. Be sure to apply little rubber stickers (e.g. with anti-slip, latex-based paint called sock stop) to the undersides of booties for babies who can stand or walk.

DIAGRAMS FOR SOLES

0-3 MONTHS

3-6 MONTHS

6-9 MONTHS

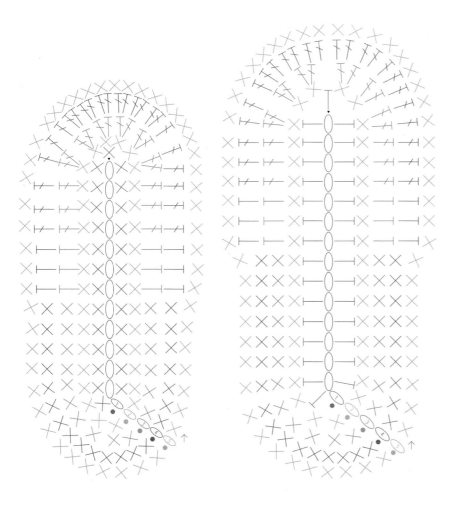

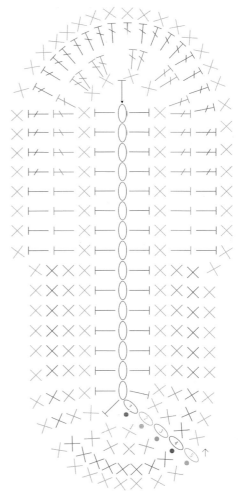

FOR LITTLE LADIES

Most ladies love shoes!
And who could blame a little
lady for wanting to follow in her mother's
footsteps from an early age?
The designs in this chapter are
ultra-chic, and will go beautifully with
your little princess's first dress.

BALLERINAS

Audrey Hepburn wore them with grace, and turned them into the must-have for every fashion-conscious lady. This classic version is guaranteed to make your lit-le lady shine!

MATERIALS

Crochet hook US B (2.5mm)
Schachenmayr original Catania
(50g/137yd/125m) in Black
(Col 110) and Cream
(Col 130), 50g each

HOW TO DO IT:

For one shoe
Start off working in rounds. Work 1 ch at the beginning of each rd, and finish the rd with 1 sl st into the first st of the rd. Do not turn work.

Rd 1: Make a magic ring and crochet 6/6/8 sc (dc) in Black yarn (6/6/8 sts).
Rd 2: *Inc 1 st, 2/2/3 sc (dc)*, rep from * to * once more (8/8/10 sts).
Rd 3: *Inc 1 st twice, 2/2/3 sc (dc)*, rep from * to * once more (12/12/14 sts).
Rd 4: 1 sc (dc), inc 1 st twice, 4/4/5 sc (dc), inc 1 st twice, 3/3/4 sc (dc) (16/16/18 sts).
Rd 5: 2 sc (dc), inc 1 st twice, 6/6/7 sc (dc), inc 1 st twice, 4/4/5 sc (dc) (20/20/22 sts).
Rd 6: 3 sc (dc), inc 1 st twice, 8/8/9 sc (dc), inc 1 st twice, 5/5/6 sc (dc) (24/24/26 sts).
Rd 7: 4 sc (dc), inc 1 st twice, 10/10/11 sc (dc), inc 1 st twice, 6/6/7 sc (dc) (28/28/30 sts).
Rd 8: 5 sc (dc), inc 1 st twice, 12/12/13 sc (dc), inc 1 st twice, 7/7/8 sc (dc) (32/32/34 sts).

Rd 9: 1 st into each st of the previous rd (32/32/34 sts).
Change yarn to Cream yarn.
Rd 10: Work into the back loop of the stitch only. 1 sc (dc) into each st of the previous rd (32/32/34 sts), 1 ch and turn work. Now continue working in rows. At the end of each row, work 1 sl st into the first st of the row, 1 turning ch, and then turn your work.
Row 11: 1 sc (dc) into each st of the previous rd (32/32/34 sts). Secure the yarn and cut. Join the Cream yarn at the 13th/13th/14th st of row 11, 1 ch and turn. Continue to work as follows:
Row 12: 26/26/28 sc (dc), do not work the last 6 sts (26/26/28 sts).
Row 13: Dec 1 st, 22/22/24 sc (dc), dec 1 st (24/24/26 sts).
Row 14: Dec 1 st, 20/20/22 sc (dc), dec 1 st (22/22/24 sts).
Row 15: 1 sc (dc) into each st of the previous row (22/22/24 sts).
Row 16: 2 sc (dc), dec 1 st, 14 sc (dc), dec 1 st, 2 sc (dc) (20/20/22 sts).
Rows 17–25/27/29: 1 sc (dc) into each st of the previous row (20/20/22 sts).
Row 26/28/30: 20/20/22 sc (dc), 4/4/2 ch (24/24/24 sts). Work in rounds again from here. Do not turn any more.
Rd 27/29/31: *2 sc (dc), dec 1 st*, rep from * to * 5 more times (18 sts).
Rd 28/30/32: *1 sc (dc), dec 1 st*, rep from * to * 5 more times (12 sts).
Rd 29/31/33: Dec 1 st 6 times (6 sts).
Rd 30/32/34: *Miss 1 st, 1 sl st*, rep from * to * twice more (3 sts).
Fasten off yarn and weave in loose ends.

FINISHING OFF

Work 1 rd of sc (dc) in Black yarn evenly around the opening of the ballerina shoe. Work 3 st tog at the inner corners of the tip of the shoe. Tie a piece of Black yarn into a little bow and sew to the front of the shoe. Repeat for the second shoe.

PEEP-TOES

So cute! Tiny toes peep out at the front, as comfortable as can be in these lovely little shoes.

MATERIALS

Crochet hook US B (2.5mm)
Schachenmayr original
Catania (50g/137yd/125m) in
Violet (Col 113), Flesh
(Col 257), 50g each, and in
White (Col 106), remnant

HOW TO DO IT:

For one shoe
Make a sole in Flesh-coloured yarn in the desired size, and continue crocheting as follows:

Rd 1: 1 back post st (bp st) in every st of the previous rd (51/55/57 sts).
Fasten off.
Join the Violet yarn to the 30th/32nd/33rd st of the last rd, and continue crocheting in rows. Work 1 ch at the end of the row and turn work.
Row 1: Work into the back loop of the stitch only. 1 sc (dc) into each of the next 38/42/44 sts (38/42/44 sts).
Row 2: Dec 1 st, 34/38/40 sc (dc), dec 1 st (36/40/42 sts).
Row 3: Dec 1 st, 32/36/38 sc (dc), dec 1 st (34/38/40 sts).
Row 4: 4/6/7 sc (dc), 10 hdc (htr), 6 dc (tr), 10 hdc (htr), 4/6/7 sc (dc) (34/38/40 sts).
Row 5: Dec 1 st, 30/34/36 sc (dc), dec 1 st (32/36/38 sts).
Row 6: Dec 1 st, 4/6/7 sc (dc), 1 hdc (htr), 18 dc (tr), 1 hdc (htr), 4/6/7 sc (dc), dec 1 st (30/34/36 sts).
Fasten off yarn.

FRONT

Join the Violet yarn to the front loop of the 28th/30th/31st st of the last rd in Flesh-coloured yarn, and continue crocheting in rows. Work 1 ch at the end of the row and turn the work.

Row 1: 8 sc (dc), dec 1 st (9 sts).
Row 2: Dec 1 st, 7 sc (dc) (8 sts).
Row 3: 6 sc (dc), dec 1 st (7 sts).
Row 4: Dec 1 st, 5 sc (dc) (6 sts).
Row 5: 4 sc (dc), dec 1 st (5 sts).
Row 6: Dec 1 st, 3 sc (dc) (4 sts).
Row 7: 2 sc (dc), dec 1 st (3 sts).
Rows 8–11: 1 sc (dc) into each st of the previous row (3 sts).
Row 12: Inc 1 st, 2 sc (dc) (4 sts).
Row 13: 3 sc (dc), inc 1 st (5 sts).
Row 14: Inc 1 st, 4 sc (dc) (6 sts).
Row 15: 5 sc (dc), inc 1 st (7 sts).
Row 16: Inc 1 st, 6 sc (dc) (8 sts).
Row 17: 7 sc (dc), inc 1 st (9 sts).
Row 18: Inc 1 st, 8 sc (dc) (10 sts).
Fasten off and leave a long yarn tail.

Sew the last row in whipstitch from the 18th/20th/21st to the 9th/11th/12th st of the last Flesh-coloured round of the sole, working into the front loops of the next 10 sts.

FRONT OPENING

To make the front opening a little smaller, rejoin the Violet yarn to the front loop of the 28th/30th/31st st of the last Flesh-coloured round of the sole. Now crochet along the row ends of the Violet front, working 2 st tog 9 times. Work 1 sl st into the front loop of the 18th/20th/21st st of the last Flesh-coloured round of the sole, 1 sl st into the next sole st, and now 1 wrong side row of sc (dc) along the row just crocheted.

Work 1 sc (dc) into each st of the previous row. Finish the row with 1 sl st into the next free st of the last round of the Flesh-coloured sole. Fasten off and weave in loose ends. Wind White yarn around the middle section of the front until it looks like a knot and fasten off securely.

FINISHING OFF

Carefully sew the row ends of the body of the shoe to the insides of the sides of the front with a few running stitches. Repeat for the second shoe

ANKLE-STRAP BALLERINAS

The classic baby shoe with a bright gold buckle and smart ankle strap is gorgeous in this cheerful turquoise.

MATERIALS

Crochet hook US B (2.5mm)
ONline Linie 165 Sandy in
Turquoise (Col 84), 50g,
Schachenmayr original Catania
(50g/137yd/125m) in Canary
(Col 208), remnant
Nylon thread in Gold and
Turquoise
Sewing needle

HOW TO DO IT:

For one shoe
Work one sole in desired size in Turquoise yarn, then continue in rounds in the same colour. Work 1 ch at the beginning of each round, and 1 sl st into the first st of the round at the end. Do not turn work.

Rd 1: 1 back post st (bp st) in every st of the previous rd (51/55/57 sts).
Rds 2–4: 1 sc (dc) into each st of the previous rd (51/55/57 sts).
Rd 5: 47/51/53 sc (dc), dec 1 st twice (49/53/55 sts).
Rd 6: 1 sc (dc) into each st of the previous rd (49/53/55 sts).
Rd 7: 17/19/20 sc (dc), dec 1 st 7 times, 18/20/21 sc (dc) (42/46/48 sts).
Rd 8: 40/44/46 sc (dc), dec 1 st (41/45/47 sts).
Rd 9: 15/17/18 sc (dc), dec 1 st twice, 3 sc (dc), dec 1 st twice, 15/17/18 sc (dc) (37/41/43 sts).
Fasten off.
Continue crocheting in rows.

ANKLE STRAPS

Left shoe
Join the Turquoise yarn to the 31st/33rd/34th st of Rd 9, and continue crocheting in rows.
Row 1: 23 ch, 1 sc (dc) into the 31st/33rd/34th st of Rd 9, 1 sc (dc) into the next 14/18/20 sc (dc).
Row 2: Dec 1 st, 13/17/19 sc (dc), 1 sc (dc) into each of the 23 ch (37/41/43 sts).
Row 3: 22 ch, 13/17/19 sc (dc), dec 1 st (36/40/42 sts).
Fasten off.

Right shoe
Join the Turquoise yarn to the 31st/33rd/34th st of Rd 9, and continue crocheting in rows.

Row 1: 15/19/21 sc (dc), 24 ch.
Row 2: 1 sc (dc) into the 2nd ch from the hook, 1 sc (dc) into each of the next 22 ch, 13/17/19 sc (dc), dec 1 st (37/41/43 sts).
Row 3: Dec 1 st, 13/17/19 sc (dc), 22 ch (36/40/42 sts).
Fasten off.

FINISHING OFF

Using Turquoise nylon thread, attach one end of the ankle strap to the opposite side. To make the buckle, crochet a small square of sl st in Canary yarn onto the top ankle strap, and backstitch a rectangle in Gold onto the crocheted buckle. Repeat for the second shoe.

MARY JANES

MATERIALS

Crochet hook US B (2.5mm)
Schachenmayr original
Catania (50g/137yd/125m) in
Cyclamen (Col 114) and
Flesh (Col 257), 50g

HOW TO DO IT:

For one shoe
Crochet a sole in desired size in Flesh-coloured yarn. Join the Cyclamen yarn to the first st of the last rd, and continue working in rounds. Close the rd with 1 sl st into the first st of the rd. Crochet 1 ch at the beginning of each rd, and do not turn the work. Note that if the instructions tell you to dec 1 st, you must dec a sc (dc) and not a dc (tr).

Rd 1: Work into the back loop of the stitch only. 1 sc (dc) into each st of the previous rd (51/55/57 sts).
Rd 2: 11/13/14 sc (dc), 25 dc (tr), 15/17/18 sc (dc) (51/55/57 sts).
Rd 3: 11/13/14 sc (dc), *1 fp dc (fp tr), 2 bp dc (bp tr)*, rep from * to * 7 times, 1 fp dc (fp tr), 15/17/18 sc (dc) (51/55/57 sts).
Rd 4: 9/11/12 sc (dc), dec 1 st, *1 fp dc (fp tr), 2 sc (dc)*, rep from * to * 7 times, 1 fp dc (fp tr), dec 1 st, 13/15/16 sc (dc) (49/53/55 sts).

Rd 5: 10/12/13 sc (dc), *1 fp dc (fp tr), dec 1 st*, rep from * to * 7 times, 1 fp dc (fp tr), 14/16/17 sc (dc) (41/45/47 sts).
Rd 6: 10/12/13 sc (dc), *1 fp dc (fp tr), 1 sc (dc)*, rep from * to * 7 times, 1 fp dc (fp tr), 12/14/15 sc (dc), dec 1 st (40/44/46 sts).
Rd 7: 8/10/11 sc (dc), dec 1 st, *1 fp dc (fp tr), miss 1 st*, rep from * to * 7 times, 1 fp dc (fp tr), dec 1 st, 11/13/14 sc (dc) (30/34/36 sts).
Do not fasten off, but continue crocheting as follows:

ANKLE STRAPS
Left shoe
Rd 8: 1 ch, turn work, 10/12/13 sc (dc), 13/14/15 ch, [1 sc (dc), 1 hdc (htr), 3 dc (tr)] into the 2nd ch from the hook, 1 hdc (htr) into the remaining 11/12/13 ch, 1 sl st into the next free st of Rd 7.
Fasten off.

Right shoe
Rd 8: 7/9/10 sc (dc), 13/14/15 ch, [1 sc (dc), 1 hdc (htr), 3 dc (tr)] into the 2nd ch from the hook, 1 hdc (htr) into each of the remaining 11/12/13 ch, 1 sl st into the 8th/10th/11th st of Rd 7.
Secure the yarn and cut.

FINISHING OFF
Attach the ankle strap to the opposite side of the shoe using the matching thread. Repeat for the second shoe.

LACE SHOES

Budding ballerinas need the right shoes. These delicate lace shoes are the perfect finishing touch to any princess's ballet outfit!

MATERIALS

Crochet hook US B (2.5mm)
Schachenmayr original Catania
(50g/137yd/125m), in Light Pink
(Col 246), 50g and Magenta
(Col 251), remnant
2 plastic beads, 4mm diameter
Textile yarn in pink, remnant
Sewing thread

HOW TO DO IT:

For one shoe
These booties are worked in rows. Start each row with 1 ch. At the end of each row, work 1 sl st into the first st of the row and turn, unless the instructions state otherwise.
Work 5/7/7 ch in Light Pink yarn.

Row 1: 1 sc (dc) into the 2nd ch from the hook, 1 sc (dc) into the next 2/4/4 ch, 3 sc (dc) into the last ch, continue working on the other side of the row of ch (do not turn): 2/4/4 sc (dc), 2 sc (dc) in the first ch with the first sc (dc) (10/14/14 sts).
Row 2: Inc 1 st twice, 2/4/4 sc (dc), inc 1 st 3 times, 2/4/4 sc (dc), inc 1 st (16/20/20 sts).
Row 3: Inc 1 st, 5/7/7 sc (dc), inc 1 st 3 times, 5/7/7 sc (dc), inc 1 st twice (22/26/26 sts). Do not turn.
Row 4: 9/11/11 sc (dc), inc 1 st twice, 9/11/11 sc (dc), inc 1 st twice (26/30/30 sts). Do not turn.
Row 5: 1 bp st into each st of the previous row (26/30/30 sts).

Rows 6–10: 1 sc (dc) into each st of the previous row (26/30/30 sts). Do not turn yet.
Secure the yarn and cut. Join the Light Pink yarn to the 7th/9th/9th st of Row 10, 1 ch and turn.
Row 11: 1 sc (dc) into each of the next 21/25/25 sc (dc) (21/25/25 sts). Do not work the last 5 st. From here, turn the work with 1 ch without working 1 sl st into the first st of the row.
Rows 12–19/23/25: 1 sc (dc) into each st of the previous row (21/25/25 sts).
Row 20/24/26: 21/25/25 sc (dc), 3/5/5 ch, 1 sl st into the first st of the row (24/30/30 sts).
Now continue working the rows as described at the beginning.
Row 21/25/27: 1 sc (dc) into each st of the previous row (24/30/30 sts).
Row 22/26/28: *2/3/3 sc (dc), dec 1 st*, rep from * to * 5 times (18/24/24 sts).
Row 23/27/29: *1/2/2 sc (dc), dec 1 st*, rep from * to * 5 times (12/18/18 sts).
Row 24/28/30: *0/1/1 sc (dc), dec 1 st*, rep from * to * 5 times (6/12/12 sts).
Row 25/29/31: *Miss 1 st, 1 sl st*, rep from * to * twice more (3 sts).
Sizes 2 and 3: dec 1 st 6 times (6 sts).
Size 1: Fasten off.
Work 1 more row for sizes 2 and 3:
Row 30/32: *Miss 1 st, 1 sl st*, rep from * to * twice more (3 sts).
Fasten off.
Join the Light Pink yarn to the edge of the shoe opening and work a row of sc (dc) around it. Dec 1 st at the two front inside edges of the shoe opening.

FINISHING OFF

Tie a small bow in the Magenta yarn and sew it to the top of the shoe. Sew a plastic bead onto the middle of the bow. Cut two pieces of textile yarn approx. 15¾in (40cm), and sew the ties on the left and right of the shoe opening as shown. Repeat for the second shoe.

Whether on sandy terrain or in the snow-covered city jungle, the boots in this chapter will always look good. And what is also guaranteed: they will keep tiny feet warm and toasty!

WILD THING!

COWBOY BOOTS

Yee-ha! Let's ride off into the sunset like real cowboys and cowgirls! These boots are an important part of any trip to the Wild West.

MATERIALS

Crochet hook US B (2.5mm) Schachenmayr original Catania (50g/137yd/125m) in Taupe (Col 254), Orchid (Col 222) and Chocolate (Col 162), 50g each, and in Cyclamen (Col 114) and Silver (Col 172), remnants

HOW TO DO IT:

For one shoe

The booties are worked in rounds. Work 1 ch at the beginning of each rd, and finish the rd with 1 sl st into the first st of the rd. Do not turn the work unless the instructions tell you to. Work one sole in desired size in Taupe yarn, then continue in rounds as follows:

Rd 1: 1 back post st (bp st) in every st of the previous rd (51/55/57 sts).
Rd 2: 1 sc (dc) into each st of the previous rd (51/55/57 sts).
Change to Orchid yarn.
Rd 3: 1 sc (dc) into each st of the previous rd (51/55/57 sts), turn.
Rd 4: 1 sc (dc) into each st of the previous rd (51/55/57 sts), turn.
Rd 5: 13/15/16 sc (dc), 20 dc (tr), 18/20/21 sc (dc) (51/55/57 sts), turn.
Rd 6: 19/21/22 sc (dc), dec 1 st 10 times, 12/14/15 sc (dc) (41/45/47 sts), turn.
Rd 7: 1 sc (dc) into each st of the previous rd (41/45/47 sts), turn.
Rd 8: 19/21/22 sc (dc), dec 1 st 5 times, 12/14/15 sc (dc) (36/40/42 sts), turn.
Rd 9: 11/13/14 sc (dc), dec 1 st twice, 1 sc (dc), dec 1 st twice, 13/15/16 sc (dc), dec 1 st, 1 sc (dc) (31/35/37 sts).
Do not turn again after this round.
Change to Chocolate yarn.

Rd 10: Work into the back loop of the stitch only. 1 sc (dc) into each st of the previous rd (31/35/37 sts).
Rds 11–15: 1 sc (dc) into each st of the previous rd (31/35/37 sts).
Rd 16: 14/16/17 sc (dc), inc 1 st, 15/17/18 sc (dc), inc 1 st (33/37/39 sts).
Rds 17 and 18: 1 sc (dc) into each st of the previous rd (33/37/39 sts).
Rd 19: 5/6/6 sc (dc), miss 1 st, 1 dc (tr), 4 dc (tr) in 1 st, 1 dc (tr), miss 1 st, 12/14/16 sc (dc), miss 1 st, 1 dc (tr), 4 dc (tr) in 1 st, 1 dc (tr), miss 1 st, 6/7/7 sc (dc) (35/39/41 sts).
Change to Cyclamen yarn.
Rds 20 and 21: 1 sc (dc) into each st of the previous rd (35/39/41 sts).
Secure the yarn and cut.

FRONT FLAP

Work in rows. Work 1 ch at the end of each row and turn the work. Join the Orchid yarn to the front loop of the 12th/14th/16th st of Rd 9, and continue crocheting as follows:

Row 1: 1 sc (dc) in the same st as you joined the yarn, 1 sc (dc) in the next 4 sts (5 sts).
Row 2: 1 sc (dc) into each st of the previous row (5 sts).
Row 3: Inc 1 st, 3 sc (dc), inc 1 st (7 sts).
Row 4: 1 sc (dc) into each st of the previous row (7 sts).
Row 5: Dec 1 st, 3 sc (dc), dec 1 st (5 sts).
Row 6: Dec 1 st, 1 sc (dc), dec 1 st (3 sts).
Secure the yarn and cut.

HEEL

Count the stitches to the 5th/7th/8th st of the last rd of the sole. Turn the work, and join the Taupe yarn into the same st. Work 1 sc (dc) into the same st as you joined the yarn, and 1 sc (dc) into the next 15/19/21 sts. Fasten off.

STAR

Rd 1: Crochet 6 sc (dc) in a magic ring in Orchid yarn (6 sc/dc).
Rd 2: 3 ch, 1 sl st into the 2nd ch from the hook, 1 sc (dc) into the next ch, 1 sc (dc) in the 2nd st of the magic ring, *3 ch, 1 sl st into the 2nd ch from the hook, 1 sc (dc) into the next ch, 1 sl st into the next st of the magic ring*, rep from * to * 3 more times, 1 sl st into the first st of the rd. Secure the yarn and cut.

SPUR

Do not start the star of the spur with a magic ring; instead, crochet 6 ch and close the ring with 1 sl st into the first ch. Then crochet the second rd as for the star (see above) by working the sl st into the ring so an opening remains in the middle of the star.

BAND

Work 43/47/49 ch in Cyclamen yarn, crochet 1 sc (dc) into the 2nd ch from the hook and 1 sc (dc) in each following ch (42/46/48 sts). Now feed the band through the opening of the silver star of the spur, and sew the ends of the band together with two whipstitches.

FINISHING OFF

Sew the star to the side of the boot using Orchid-coloured thread. Sew the rim of the front flap to the boot in Orchid yarn using running stitches. Slide the spur band over the boot opening and secure. Repeat for the second shoe.

HIPPY BOOTS

These fringed booties are hip and fun – perfect with warm tights and a warm skirt.

MATERIALS

Crochet hook US B (2.5mm)
Schachenmayr original
Catania (50g/137yd/125m)
in Flesh (Col 257) and
Cream (Col 130), 50g each

HOW TO DO IT:

For one shoe

The booties are worked in rounds. Work 1 ch at the beginning of the round, and finish the round with 1 sl st into the first st of the rd. Do not turn the work. Work one sole in desired size in Flesh yarn, then continue as follows in the same colour:

Rd 1: 1 back post st (bp st) in every st of the previous rd (51/55/57 sts). Change yarn to Cream yarn.

Rds 2–4: 1 sc (dc) into each st of the previous rd (51/55/57 sts).

Rd 5: 18/20/21 sc (dc), dec 1 st twice, 4 sc (dc), dec 1 st twice, 21/23/24 sc (dc) (47/51/53 sts).

Rd 6: 19/21/22 sc (dc), dec 1 st, 2 sc (dc), dec 1 st, 22/24/25 sc (dc) (45/49/51 sts).

Rd 7: 18/20/21 sc (dc), 1 hdc (htr), 4 dc (tr), 1 hdc (htr), 21/23/24 sc (dc) (45/49/51 sts).

Rd 8: 15/17/18 sc (dc), dec 1 st twice, 4 dc (tr), dec 1 st twice, 16/18/19 sc (dc), dec 1 st (40/44/46 sts).

Rd 9: 14/16/17 sc (dc), dec 1 st 5 times, 16/18/19 sc (dc) (35/39/41 sts).

Rd 10: 12/14/15 sc (dc), 2 hdc (htr), 5 dc (tr), 2 hdc (htr), 14/16/17 sc (dc) (35/39/41 sts).

Rd 11: 12/14/15 sc (dc), dec 1 st, 5 sc (dc), dec 1 st, 14/16/17 sc (dc) (33/37/39 sts).

Rd 12: 11/13/14 sc (dc), dec 1 st, 5 sc (dc), dec 1 st, 13/15/16 sc (dc) (31/35/37 sts).

Rd 13: 9 ch, 1 sc (dc) in the first st of the rd, *1 sl st into the next st, 9 ch, 1 sc (dc) into the same st that you worked the last sl st*, rep from * to * another 29/33/35 times, 1 sl st into the first sc (dc) of the rd and not the ch (31/35/37 sts; count the sc (dc) only).

Rd 14: 1 sc (dc) into each sc (dc) of the previous rd. (miss the sl st and ch arches) (31/35/37 sts).

Rds 15 and 16: 1 sc (dc) into each st of the previous rd (31/35/37 sts).

Rd 17: 9 ch, 1 sc (dc) in the first st of the rd, *1 sl st into the next st, 9 ch, 1 sc (dc) into the same st that you worked the last sl st*, rep from * to * another 29/33/35 times, 1 sl st into the first sc (dc) of the rd and not the ch (31/35/37 sts; count the sc (dc) only).

Rd 18: 1 sc (dc) into each sc (dc) of the previous round (miss the sl st and ch arches) (31/35/37 sts).

Rds 19 and 20: 1 sc (dc) into each st of the previous rd (31/35/37 sts).

Rd 21: 9 ch, 1 sc (dc) in the first st of the rd, *1 sl st into the next st, 9 ch, 1 sc (dc) into the same st that you worked the last sl st*, rep from * to * another 29/33/35 times, 1 sl st into the first sc (dc) of the rd and not the ch (31/35/37 sts; count the sc (dc) only).

Rd 22: 1 sc (dc) into each sc (dc) of the previous rd (miss the sl st and ch arches) (31/35/37 sts). Turn work after this rd.

Rd 23: 1 sc (dc) into each st of the previous rd (31/35/37 sts). Fasten off. Repeat for the second shoe.

FUR BOOTS

MATERIALS

Crochet hook US B (2.5mm)
Schachenmayr original
Catania (50g/137yd/125m)
in Marigold (Col 383) and
Flesh (Col 257), 50g each,
and in Cream
(Col 130), remnant
2 wooden buttons, natural
look, 20mm diameter

HOW TO DO IT:

For one shoe

Work one sole in desired size in Marigold yarn, then continue in rounds in the same colour. Work 1 ch at the beginning of each rd, and at the end 1 sl st into the first st of the rd. Do not turn work unless the instructions tell you to.

LEFT AND RIGHT BOOTS

Rd 1: Work into the back loop of the stitch only. 1 sc (dc) into each st of the previous rd (51/55/57 sts).

Rd 2: 1 sc (dc) into each st of the previous rd (51/55/57 sts).
Change colour to Flesh-coloured yarn, 1 ch and turn work.

Rd 3: 1 sc (dc) into each st of the previous rd (51/55/57 sts), 1 ch and turn work.

Rd 4: 18/20/21 sc (dc), dec 1 st, 5 sc (dc), dec 1 st, 24/26/27 sc (dc) (49/53/55 sts). Do not turn the work.

Rd 5: 19/21/22 sc (dc), dec 1 st, 1 sc (dc), dec 1 st, 23/25/26 sc (dc), dec 1 st (46/50/52 sts).

Rd 6: 14/16/17 sc (dc), dec 1 st 3 times, 1 sc (dc), dec 1 st 3 times, 16/18/19 sc (dc), dec 1 st, 1 sc (dc) (39/43/45 sts).

Rd 7: Dec 1 st, 11/13/14 sc (dc), dec 1 st twice, 1 sc (dc), dec 1 st twice, 14/16/17 sc (dc), dec 1 st, 1 sc (dc) (33/37/39 sts).

Rd 8: 11/13/14 sc (dc), dec 1 st, crochet 3 st tog, dec 1 st, 15/17/18 sc (dc) (29/33/35 sts).

Rd 9 and 10: 1 sc (dc) into each st of the previous rd (29/33/35 sts), 1 ch and turn work.

Rd 11: 1 sc (dc) into each st of the previous rd (29/33/35 sts).
Fasten off and continue working in the 12th row for the shoe. The rest of the shoe is worked in rows. Crochet 1 ch and turn at the end of each row.

Right boot

Join the Flesh yarn to the front loop of the 23rd/27th/29th st of Rd 11 and continue crocheting as follows. 1 ch and turn work.

Row 12: Work 4 sc (dc) into the back loop of the stitch only, work 25/29/31 sc (dc) into both loops of the stitch, work 4 sc (dc) into the front loop of the stitch only (the same 4 st as at the beginning of the row) (33/37/39 sts).

Rows 13–16: 1 sc (dc) into each st of the previous row (33/37/39 sts).

Row 17: 31/35/37 sc (dc), dec 1 st (32/36/38 sts).

Row 18: 1 sc (dc) into each st of the previous row (32/36/38 sts).

Row 19: 30/34/36 sc (dc), dec 1 st (31/35/37 sts).

Row 20: 1 sc (dc) into each st of the previous row (31/35/37 sts).

Row 21: Dec 1 st, 27/31/33 sc (dc), dec 1 st (29/33/35 sts).

Row 22: Dec 1 st, 25/29/31 sc (dc), dec 1 st (27/31/33 sts).
Secure the yarn and cut.

Left boot

Join the Flesh-coloured yarn to the back loop of the 8th st of Rd 11 and continue crocheting as follows:
1 ch and turn work.

Row 12: Work 4 sc (dc) into the front loop of the stitch only, work 25/29/31 sc (dc) into both loops of the stitch, work 4 sc (dc) into the back loop of the stitch only (the same 4 st as at the beginning of the row) (33/37/39 sts).

Rows 13–16: 1 sc (dc) into each st of the previous row (33/37/39 sts).

Row 17: Dec 1 st, 31/35/37 sc (dc) (32/36/38 sts).

Row 18: 1 sc (dc) into each st of the previous row (32/36/38 sts).

Row 19: Dec 1 st, 30/36/38 sc (dc) (31/35/37 sts).

Row 20: 1 sc (dc) into each st of the previous row (31/35/37 sts).

Row 21: Dec 1 st, 27/31/33 sc (dc), dec 1 st (29/33/35 sts).

Row 22: Dec 1 st, 25/29/31 sc (dc), dec 1 st (27/31/33 sts).
Fasten off.

FUR SURROUND (BOTH BOOTS)

Join the Cream yarn to the last st of the 12th row and crochet around the top of the shoe, working 1 tulip st at the end of each row and into each st.

FINISHING OFF

Sew the button onto the side at the 18th row of the shoe. Crochet the loop at the same height on the opposite part of the side opening. Rejoin the Flesh-coloured yarn and crochet 20 ch. Secure the row of ch with a sl st at the position where you rejoined the yarn. Adjust the quantity of ch according to the desired width of the shoe opening.

SPORTY & CHEEKY

Sneakers and trainers are absolutely on trend, and go with any outfit. But make sure your little one doesn't run away in them!

TRAINERS

Even if your baby isn't yet able to walk, they'll look good in these sporty sneakers. Style your personal trainer – and don't be afraid to use colour!

MATERIALS

Crochet hook US B (2.5mm)
Schachenmayr original Catania
(50g/137yd/125m) in Black
(Col 110), White (Col 106)
and Light Blue (Col 173), 50g
each, and ONline Linie 165
Sandy (Col 173), 50g and
ONline Linie 55 Montego
(Col 24), remnant
Embroidery needle

HOW TO DO IT:

For one shoe

Work one sole in desired size in Black yarn. Change to White yarn at the end of the round, and continue working in rounds as follows:

Rd 1: Work into the back loop of the stitch only. 1 sc (dc) into each st of the previous rd (51/55/57 sts).

Rd 2: 1 sc (dc) into each st of the previous rd (51/55/57 sts).
Change to Black yarn.

Rd 3: Work into the back loop of the stitch only. 1 sc (dc) into each st of the previous rd (51/55/57 sts).

Rd 4: 3 ch (as the first dc/tr), 2 dc (tr), [1 dc (tr) and 1 hdc (htr)] in 1 st, 6/8/9 sc (dc), 1 hdc (htr), 2 dc (tr), 1 hdc (htr), 18 sc (dc), 1 hdc (htr), 2 sc (tr), 1 hdc (htr), 6/8/9 sc (dc), [1 hdc (htr) and 1 dc (tr)] in 1 st, 8 sc (tr). 1 sl st in the 3rd ch of the first dc (tr) in the rd (53/57/59 sts).

Rd 5: 1 sc (dc) into each st of the previous rd (53/57/59 sts). Change to Turquoise yarn.

Rd 6: Work into the back loop of the stitch only. 15/17/18 sc (dc), change to White yarn, 3 sc (dc), dec 1 st 6 times, 3 sc (dc), change to Turquoise yarn, 16/18/19 sc (dc), dec 1 st twice (45/49/51 sts).

Rd 7: 16/18/19 sc (dc), change to White, dec 1 st, 6 dc (tr), dec 1 st, change to Turquoise yarn, 19/21/22 sc (dc) (43/47/49 sts).

Rd 8: 17/19/20 sc (dc), change to White, dec 1 st 3 times, change to Turquoise yarn, 20/22/23 sc (dc) (40/44/46 sts).

Rd 9: 15/17/18 sc (dc), 7 dc (tr), 18/20/21 sc (dc) (40/44/46 sts).

Rd 10: 13/15/16 sc (dc), dec 1 st twice, 5 dc (tr), dec 1 st twice, 14/16/17 sc (dc) (36/40/42 sts).

Rd 11: 9/11/12 sc (dc), 2 hdc (htr) in 1 st, 3 sc (dc), dec 1 st, 7 sc (dc), dec 1 st, 3 sc (dc), 2 hdc (htr) in 1 st, 8/10/11 sc (dc) (36/40/42 sts). Change to White yarn.

Rd 12: 4 hdc (htr), 5/7/8 sc (dc), 2 hdc (htr) in 1 st twice, dec 1 st twice, work into front loop of st only: 7 sc (dc), work into both loop of st again: dec 1 st twice, 2 hdc (htr) in 1 st twice, 5/7/8 sc (dc), 3 hdc (htr) (36/40/42 sts). Fasten off.
Join the Light Blue yarn to the front loop of the 35th/39th/41st st of Rd 12 and continue crocheting in rows. Work 1 ch at the end of the rd and turn work.

Rows 1–4: 4 sc (dc) (4 sts).
Fasten off. Fold the crocheted piece down the middle, and sew the last row to the last round of the shoe using whipstitch.

FLAP

Join the Turquoise yarn to the back loop of the 15th st of Rd 11 and continue crocheting in rows. Work 1 ch at the end of the row and turn.

Row 1: Inc 1 st, 5 sc (dc), inc 1 st (9 sts).

Row 2: 1 sc (dc) into each st of the previous row (9 sts).

Row 3: Inc 1 st, 7 sc (dc), inc 1 st (11 sts).

Rows 4–6: 1 sc (dc) into each st of the previous row (11 sts). Fasten off.

SYMBOL

Work 9 ch in Light Blue yarn. Work 1 sl st into the 2nd ch from the hook, 1 sl st, 2 sc (dc), 2 dc (tr), work 2 dc (tr) tog, 4 ch, 1 sl st into the 2nd ch from the hook, 2 sc (dc) into 1 ch, [1 sc (dc), 1 hdc (htr), 1 dc (tr)] into 1 ch, 1 sl st into the very first ch. Sew the symbol onto the side of the shoe using running stitch.

BACK PART OF THE SHOE (THICK HEEL)

Join the White yarn to the front loop of the 38th/42nd/44th st of Rd 2 of the shoe, and continue crocheting as follows:

Row 1: 1 sl st into the st where you joined the yarn, 2 sc (dc), 2 hdc (htr), 13 dc (tr), 2 hdc (htr), 2 sc (dc), 1 sl st. Fasten off and leave a long yarn tail. Use the yarn tail to attach the item with running stitches.

FRONT PART OF THE SHOE

Join the Black yarn to the front loop of the 20th/22nd/23rd st of the last rd of the sole, and continue crocheting in rows. Work 1 ch at the end of the row and turn work.

Row 1: Dec 1 st, 2 sc (dc), dec 1 st (4 sts).

Row 2: 1 sc (dc) into each st of the previous row (4 sts)
Fasten off. Sew the item onto the shoe using running stitch.

SHOELACE

Use an embroidery needle to thread the neon yellow yarn through the stitches like a shoelace. Repeat for the second shoe.

BASKETBALL SHOES

Always stay cool! This classic shoe belongs in every wardrobe because it goes with any outfit.

MATERIALS

Crochet hook US B (2.5mm)
Schachenmayr Catania
(50g/137yd/125m) in Blue
Iris (Col 384) and White
(Col 106), 50g each, length of
yarn in Black to sew
on to the star

HOW TO DO IT:

For one shoe
Work one sole in desired size in White yarn. Work in rows. Follow the instructions closely (sl st and turn).

BASE

Row 1: 1 back post st (bp st) in each st of the previous rd, 1 sl st into the 1st st of the rd, turn (51/55/57 sts).
Row 2: 1 sc (dc) in each st of the previous rd, 1 sl st into the 1st st of the rd, turn (51/55/57 sts).
Row 3: 1 sc (dc) in each st of the previous rd, 1 sl st into the 1st st of the rd (51/55/57 sts). Secure the yarn and cut. Do not turn the work. Miss 21/23/24 sts of the previous rd, and join the White yarn.
Row 4: Work into the front loop of the stitch only. 3 sc (dc), 1 sl st, 1 ch and turn work (4 sts).
Row 5: 4 sc (dc), 1 sc (dc) into the back loop of the next st of Row 3, 1 sl st into the back loop of the next st, 1 ch and turn (6 sts).
Row 6: 6 sc (dc), 1 sc (dc) into the front loop of the st of Row 3, 1 sl st into the front loop of the next st, 1 ch and turn (8 sts).

Row 7: 8 sc (dc), 1 sc (dc) into the back loop of the next st of Row 3, 1 sl st into the back loop of the next st, 1 ch and turn (10 sts).
Row 8: 10 sc (dc), 1 sc (dc) into the front loop of the st of Row 3, 1 sl st into the front loop of the next st, 1 ch and turn (12 sts).
Row 9: 12 sc (dc), 1 sc (dc) into the back loop of the next st of Row 3, 1 sl st into the back loop of the next st, 1 ch and turn (14 sts).
Row 10: 14 sc (dc), 1 sc (dc) into the front loop of the st of Row 3, 1 sl st into the front loop of the next st (16 sts). Secure the yarn and cut.
For the flap, miss the first 18/20/21 sts of Row 3. Join the Capri yarn at the 19th/21st/22nd st. Work in rows. Work 1 ch at the end of the row and turn work).

Rows 1–13: 10 sc (dc) (10 sts).
Row 14: Dec 1 st, 6 sc (dc), dec 1 st (8 sts).
Row 15: Dec 1 st, 4 sc (dc), dec 1 st (6 sts).
Row 16: Dec 1 st 3 times (3 sts).
Fasten off. Join the Capri yarn to the next st to the left of the flap and continue working in rows as follows:

Row 1: Work into the back loop of the stitch only. 1 sc (dc) into each free st of Row 3 of the base (41/45/47 sts).
Rows 2 and 3: 1 sc (dc) into each st of the previous row (41/45/47 sts).
Row 4: Dec 1 st, 37/41/43 sc (dc), dec 1 st (39/43/45 sts).
Row 5: Dec 1 st, 35/39/41 sc (dc), dec 1 st (37/41/43 sts).
Row 6: Dec 1 st, 33/37/39 sc (dc), dec 1

st (35/39/41 sts).
Row 7: Dec 1 st, 31/35/37 sc (dc), dec 1 st (33/37/39 sts).
Row 8: Dec 1 st, 29/33/35 sc (dc), dec 1 st (31/35/37 sts).
Rows 9 and 10: 1 sc (dc) into each st of the previous row (31/35/37 sts).
Fasten off.

CIRCLE

Work in rounds. Start each round with 1 ch, and finish each round with 1 sl st into the 1st st. Do not turn the work.

Rd 1: Crochet 6 sc (dc) in a magic ring in White yarn (6 sts). Secure the yarn and cut. Use White yarn to sew the circle onto the side of the shoe using running stitch and embroider a star onto the middle of the circle using Black yarn.

SHOELACES

Work 120 ch in White yarn.

FINISHING OFF

Carefully thread the laces through either side of the shoe front and tie a bow at the top. Repeat for the second shoe.

HIKING BOOTS

Your little darling will be able to climb every mountain in these practical hiking boots. No hill is too high, no challenge too great. Let the adventure begin!

MATERIALS

Crochet hooks US B (2.5mm) for the shoes, and US J (6mm) for the laces only Schachenmayr original Catania (50g/137yd/125m) in Black (Col 110) and Canary (Col 208), 50g each, and in Gold (Col 249), remnant

HOW TO DO IT:

For one shoe
Work one sole in desired size in Black yarn, then work in rounds in the same colour. At the end of the round, work 1 sl st into the first st of the rd, and 1 ch at the beginning of the new rd.

Rd 1: 1 back post st (bp st) in each st of the previous rd (51/55/57 sts).
Change to Gold yarn.
Rd 2: Work into the back loop of the stitch only. 1 sc (dc) into each st of the previous rd (51/55/57 sts).
Change to Canary yarn.
Rd 3: 1 sc (dc) into each st of the previous rd (51/55/57 sts).
Rd 4: 47/51/53 sc (dc), dec 1 st twice (49/53/55 sts).
Rd 5: 16/18/19 sc (dc), 14 dc (tr), 19/21/22 sc (dc) (49/53/55 sts).
Rds 6 and 7: 1 sc (dc) into each st of the previous rd (49/53/55 sts).
Rd 8: 16/18/19 sc (dc), dec 1 st 7 times, 19/21/22 sc (dc) (42/46/48 sts).
Rd 9: 15/17/18 sc (dc), dec 1 st twice, 1 sc (dc), dec 1 st twice, 18/20/21 sc (dc) (38/42/44 sts).

Rd 10: 13/15/16 sc (dc), dec 1 st, 7 sc (dc), dec 1 st, 14/16/17 sc (dc) (36/40/42 sts).
Fasten off.

ANKLE

Continue working in rows. Work 1 ch at the end of each row and turn work.

Row 1: Join the yarn in Canary to the front loop of the 22nd/24th/25th st of Rd 10. Work into the front loop of the stitch only. Crochet 1 sc (dc) into 29/33/35 sts (29/33/35 sts).
Row 2: Miss 1 st, 27/31/33 sc (dc), 1 sl st (28/32/34 sts).
Row 3: Miss 1 st, 27/31/33 sc (dc) (27/31/33 sts).
Rows 4–10/12/13: 1 sc (dc) into each st of the previous row (27/31/33 sts).
Fasten off.
Now join the Gold yarn to the 1st st of Row 1 of the ankle, and crochet 1 sc (dc) into the end of each row. Then, along the top of the shaft, work 1 fp dc (fp tr) into each st of Row 10/12/13. Then crochet 1 sc (dc) into the end of each row and down to the last st of the 1st ankle row. Finish the last st with 1 additional sl st. Fasten off.

FLAP

Row 1: Join the yarn to the back loop of the 13th/15th/16th st of Row 10. Work 2 sc (dc) into the back loop of the stitch only, work 3 st tog, 2 sc (dc) into both loops of the stitch, work 2 sc (dc) into the back loop only (9 sts).
Rows 2–6: 1 sc (dc) into each st of the previous row (9 sts).
Row 7: Inc 1 st, 7 sc (dc), inc 1 st

(11 sts).
Rows 8 and 9: 1 sc (dc) into each st of the previous row (11 sts).
Row 10: Inc 1 st, 9 sc (dc), inc 1 st (13 sts).
Row 11/11–13/11–14: 1 sc (dc) into each st of the previous row (13 sts).
Fasten off.

LACES

Using Gold and Black yarn held double, crochet a length of 90/110/110 ch. Secure the ends, and trim as short as possible. Carefully thread the laces through each side of the shoe front. Repeat for the second shoe.

The sun is smiling
and baby is too!
Little feet will be happy in
these chic summer shoes.
Bring on the summer!

SUMMER, SUN & SANDALS

GARDEN SHOES

These comfortable shoes are perfect for a casual yet sporty appearance, whether at home, on the beach or working in the garden.

MATERIALS

Crochet hook US B (2.5mm)
Schachenmayr original
Catania (50g/137yd/125m)
in Sea Green (Col 241), 50g,
4 buttons (with a motif of
choice), 15mm diameter
Sewing thread to
match buttons

HOW TO DO IT:

For one shoe
Make a sole in the desired size in Sea Green yarn, and continue crocheting as follows:

Rd 1: Work into the back loop of the stitch only. 1 hdc (htr) in each st of the previous rd (51/55/57 sts).
Work 1 ch and turn.
Rd 2: 1 hdc (htr) in each st of the previous rd (51/55/57 sts). Work 1 ch and turn.
Rd 3: 11/13/14 sc (dc), 25 dc (tr), 15/17/18 sc (dc) (51/55/57 sts).
Do not turn work.
Rd 4: 1 hdc (htr) into each st of the previous rd (51/55/57 sts).
Fasten off.

Continue working in rows only. Work 1 ch at the end of the row and turn work.

Join the Sea Green yarn to the 8th/10th/11th st of Row 3:

Row 1: 8 sc (dc), *crochet 2 hdc (htr) tog, 1 ch, miss 2 st*, rep from * to * 3 more times, crochet 2 hdc (htr) tog, 8 sc (dc) (25 sts).
Row 2: Dec 1 st twice, 4 sc (dc), 1 sc (dc) into the length of ch, *sc (dc), 1 sc (dc) into the length of ch*, rep from * to * twice more, 6 sc (dc), dec 1 st twice (21 sts).
Row 3: Dec 1 st, 2 sc (dc), *miss 1 st, crochet 2 hdc (htr) tog*, rep from * to * 3 more times, miss 1 st, 2 sc (dc), dec 1 st (10 sts).
Row 4: Dec 1 st 5 times (5 sts).
Row 5: 1 hdc (htr) into each st of the previous row (5 sts).
Fasten off.

STRAPS

Work 31/33/34 ch in Sea Green yarn. 1 sc (dc) into the 2nd ch from the hook, 1 sc (dc) in each of the next 28/30/31 ch, 5 sc (dc) into the last ch. Now continue working on the other side of the length of ch: 28/30/31 sc (dc), 4 sc (dc) into the same st as you worked the first sc (dc) at the beginning. Close the rd with 1 sl st into the first st of the rd (66/70/72 sts). Secure each end of the strap on the left and right of the shoe with a button. Repeat for the second shoe.

STRAPPY SANDALS

Why not crochet these wonderfully light and airy sandals for your little one to wear on lovely, warm summer days!

MATERIALS

Crochet hook US B (2.5mm)
Schachenmayr original
Catania (50g/137yd/125m)
in Flesh (Col 257), Light
Pink (Col 246) and Magenta
(Col 251), 50g each
2 pink rocaille beads,
2mm diameter
2 rivets (ideally shaped like
flowers), diameter 7mm
Sewing needle, pink
sewing thread

HOW TO DO IT:

For one shoe

Crochet 1 sole for each shoe in desired size in Light Pink and Flesh-coloured yarn. Place the soles together with the wrong sides facing. Hold your work so that you are looking at the Light Pink sole from above, and now crochet the two soles together with 1 rd of sl st in Pale Pink yarn (51/55/57 sts).

FRONT PART OF SANDAL

Count the st of the last Light Pink rd to the 18th/20th/21st st, then turn and now join Magenta yarn to the back loop of this st. Continue working in rows. Work 1 ch at the end of each row and turn work.

Row 1: 1 sc (dc) into the same st as you joined the yarn, 1 sc (dc) into each of the next 8/8/9 sts (9/9/10 sts).
Row 2: 1 sc (dc) into each st of the previous row (9/9/10 sts).
Row 3: Dec 1 st, 5/5/6 sc (dc), dec 1 st (7/7/8 sts).

Row 4: Dec 1 st, 5/5/6 sc (dc) (6/6/7 sts).
Row 5: 4/4/5 sc (dc), dec 1 st (5/5/6 sts).
Row 6: 1 sc (dc) into each st of the previous row (5/5/6 sts).
Row 7: 3/3/4 sc (dc), dec 1 st (4/4/5 sts).
Rows 8–10: 1 sc (dc) into each st of the previous row (4/4/5 sts).
Row 11: 3/3/4 sc (dc), inc 1 st (5/5/6 sts).
Row 12: 1 sc (dc) into each st of the previous row (5/5/6 sts).
Row 13: 4/4/5 sc (dc), inc 1 st (6/6/7 sts).
Row 14: Inc 1 st, 5/5/6 sc (dc) (7/7/8 sts).
Row 15: Inc 1 st, 5/5/6 sc (dc), inc 1 st (9/9/10 sts).
Rows 16 and 17: 1 sc (dc) into each st of the previous row (9/9/10 sts).
Now place the work tog so that the 1st st of Row 17 is on the 29th/31st/32nd st of the last Light Pink rd of the sole, and crochet the two pieces tog with 9/9/10 sl st in Magenta yarn.

BOW

Work in rows. Work 1 ch at the end of each row and turn work.

Part 1

Row 1: Work 6 ch in Magenta yarn. Work 1 sc (dc) in the 2nd ch from the hook, and 1 sc (dc) into the remaining 4 ch (5 sts).
Rows 2–28: 1 sc (dc) into each st of the previous row(5 sts).
Join the first and last row with sl st. Secure the yarn and cut.

Part 2

Row 1: Work 11 ch in Magenta yarn. Work 1 sc (dc) in the 2nd ch from the hook, and 1 sc (dc) into the remaining 9 ch (10 sts).
Row 2: 1 sc (dc) into each st of the previous row (10 sts).
Fasten off, leaving a long yarn tail. Wrap Part 2 around the middle of Part 1 to make a bow. Using Magenta yarn, sew the ends of part 2 tog in whipstitch, then sew the bow to the middle of the front part of the sandal.
Repeat for the second shoe.

BACK OF THE SANDAL (STRAP)

RIGHT SHOE

Work in rows. Work 1 ch at the end of each row and turn the work. Count the st of the last pink rd to the 43rd/47th/49th st, then turn and now join Magenta yarn to the back loop of this new st.

Left strap (A)

Row 1: Sc (dc) into the same st where you cast on, 1 sc (dc) into the next st (2 sts).
Rows 2–5: 1 sc (dc) into each st of the previous row (2 sts).
Row 6: Inc 1 st, 1 sc (dc) (3 sts).
Fasten off.
Count the st of the last Light Pink rd to the 5th st, then turn and now join Magenta yarn to the back loop of this new st.

Right strap and ankle strap (B)

Row 1: Sc (dc) into the same st where you cast on, 1 sc (dc) into the next st (2 sts).
Rows 2–5: 1 sc (dc) into each st of the previous row (2 sts).

Row 6: 1 sc (dc), inc 1 st (3 sts).

Row 7: 2 sc (dc), inc 1 st (4 sts). Do not fasten off, but continue crocheting as follows: 9 ch, *inc 1 st, 2 sc (dc)* (rep from * to * in the last row of A), 20/22/24 ch.

Row 8: 1 sc (dc) into the 2nd ch from the hook, 1 sc (dc) into each of the next 18/20/ 22 ch, 4 sc (dc) into the last row of (A), 9 sc (dc) into the line of ch, 4 sc (dc) into the last row of (B). Work 1 ch and turn.

Row 9: 1 sc (dc), dec 1 st, 11 sc (dc), dec 1 st, 18/20/22 sc (dc), dec 1 st. Fasten off.

BACK OF THE SANDAL (STRAP)

LEFT SHOE

Work in rows. Work 1 ch at the end of each row and turn the work. Count the st of the last pink rd to the 5th st, then turn and now join Magenta yarn to the back loop of this new st.

Right strap (A)

Row 1: Sc (dc) into the same st where you cast on, 1 sc (dc) into the next st (2 sts).

Rows 2–5: 1 sc (dc) into each st of the previous row (2 sts).

Row 6: 1 sc (dc), inc 1 st (3 sts). Secure the yarn and cut.

Count the st of the last pink rd to the 43rd/47th/49th st, then turn and now join Magenta yarn to the back loop of this new st.

Left strap and ankle strap (B)

Row 1: 1 sc (dc) into the same st where you cast on, 1 sc (dc) into the next st (2 sts).

Rows 2–5: 1 sc (dc) into each st of the previous row (2 sts).

Row 6: Inc 1 st, 1 sc (dc) (3 sts).

Row 7: Inc 1 st, 2 sc (dc) (4 sts). Fasten off. Turn work, and rejoin the yarn at the last st of the row, then continue crocheting as follows:

Row 1: 9 ch, *inc 1 st, 2 sc (dc)* (rep from * to * in the last row of A), 20/22/24 ch.

Row 2: 1 sc (dc) into the 2nd ch from the hook, 1 sc (dc) into each of the next 18/20/22 ch, 4 sc (dc) into the last row of (A), 9 sc (dc) into the line of ch, 4 sc (dc) into the last row of (B). Work 1 ch and turn.

Row 3: 1 sc (dc), dec 1 st, 11 sc (dc), dec 1 st, 18/20/22 sc (dc), dec 1 st. Fasten off.

Using fine pink sewing thread, attach the loose end of the strap to the top of the strap with a few stitches. Decorate the closure with a rivet. Insert the needle and thread through the back of the crocheted strap, then through the opening in the rivet, and then through a rocaille bead. Push the needle through the rivet and the strap again. Knot the thread and neaten the end.

FLIP-FLOPS

Flip-flops are the ultimate summer accessory! So why shouldn't our little ones have their own version? These shoes are perfect with shorts or a summer dress.

MATERIALS

Crochet hook US B (2.5mm)
Schachenmayr original
Catania (50g/137yd/125m)
in Flesh (Col 257), Canary
(Col 208) and Taupe
(Col 254), 50g each

HOW TO DO IT:

For one shoe

Crochet 1 sole in desired size for each shoe in Flesh-coloured and Canary yarns. Place the soles together with the wrong sides facing, and work 1 round of sc (dc) around them in Flesh yarn with the Canary side facing you. Insert the hook into the back loop only of the sole in Canary yarn, and into the front loop only of the sole in Flesh-coloured yarn. Close the rd with 1 sl st into the first st of the rd. Fasten off.

Join the yarn in Taupe to the front loop of the 5th st of the last round of the sole in Canary yarn, and continue crocheting as follows:

Row 1: 15/17/18 ch, 1 sl st into the 16th/18th/19th st (for the left shoe; for the right shoe: into the 21st/23rd/24th st) of Rd 3 of the sole in Canary yarn, 15/17/18 ch, 1 sl st into the 42nd/46th/48th st of the last rd, 12 ch, 1 sl st into the same st where you joined the new yarn at the beginning. Work 1 ch and turn.
Row 2: 1 sc (dc) into each ch of the previous row, 1 sl st into the sl st of the previous row, 1 sc (dc) into each additional ch of the previous row, 1 sl st into the sl st of the previous row, 1 sc (dc) into each ch of the previous row. 1 sl st into the first st of the row.
Fasten off and weave in loose ends.
Repeat for the second shoe.

ESPADRILLES

These shoes are perfect for girls and boys. Why not crochet a whole range of them for your little darling, in stripes or just plain.

MATERIALS

Crochet hook US B (2.5mm)
Schachenmayr Catania
(50g/137yd/125m) in Flesh
(Col 257), Canary (Col 208),
Cyclamen (Col 114), Red
(Col 115) and Tangerine
(Col 209), 50g each

HOW TO DO IT:

For one shoe

Work one sole in desired size in Flesh-coloured yarn, then continue in rounds as follows:

Rd 1: 1 back post st (bp st) in each st of the previous rd (51/55/57 sts).
Rd 2: 1 fp dc (fp tr) into each st of the previous rd (51/55/57 sts).
Fasten off.
Join the Cyclamen yarn to the 37th/41st/43rd st of the previous rd. Continue working in rows. Work 1 ch at the end of each row and turn the work.

Row 1: Work into the back loop of the stitch only. 1 sc (dc) into each of the next 25 sts (26 sts). Change to Canary yarn.
Row 2: Work into the front loop of the stitch only. 1 sc (dc) into each st of the previous row (25 sts). Change to Red yarn.
Row 3: Work into the back loop of the stitch only. 1 sc (dc) into each st of the previous row (25 sts). Change to Tangerine yarn.
Row 4: Work into the front loop of the stitch only. 1 sc (dc) into each st of the previous row (25 sts). Change to Cyclamen yarn.
Row 5: Work into the back loop of the stitch only:
1 sc (dc) into each st of the previous row (25 sts). Fasten off.

FRONT OF SHOE

Work in rows. Crochet 1 ch at the end of each row and turn work.

0-3 months
Row 1 (top): Work 21 ch in Cyclamen yarn. Work 1 sc (dc) in the 2nd ch from the hook, and 1 sc (dc) into each of the remaining 19 ch (20 sts). Change to Canary yarn.
Row 2: Work into the front loop of the st only. 1 sc (dc) into each st of the previous row (20 sts). Change to Red yarn.
Row 3: 1 sc (dc) into each st of the previous row (20 sts). Change to Tangerine yarn.
Row 4: Work into the front loop of the stitch only. 1 sc (dc) into each st of the previous row (20 sts). Change to Cyclamen yarn.
Row 5: 1 sc (dc) into each st of the previous row (20 sts). Change to Canary yarn.
Row 6: Work into the front loop of the st only. 1 sc (dc) into each st of the previous row (20 sts). Change to Cyclamen yarn.
Row 7: Dec 1 st, 6 sc (dc), dec 1 st twice, 6 sc (dc), dec 1 st (16 sts). Change to Tangerine yarn.
Row 8: Work into the front loop of the stitch only. 1 sc (dc) into each st of the previous row (16 sts). Change to Red yarn.
Row 9: Dec 1 st, 4 sc (dc), dec 1 st twice, 4 sc (dc), dec 1 st (12 sts). Change to Canary yarn.
Row 10: Work into the front loop of the stitch only. Dec 1 st, 2 sc (dc), dec 1 st twice, 2 sc (dc), dec 1 st (8 sts). Change to Cyclamen yarn.
Row 11: Work into the back loop of the stitch only. Dec 1 st 4 times (4 sts). Change to Tangerine yarn.
Row 12: Work into the front loop of the st only. Dec 1 st twice (2 sts).
Fasten off.

3-6 months
Row 1 (top): Work 21 ch in Red yarn. Work 1 sc (dc) in the 2nd ch from the hook, and 1 sc (dc) into each of the remaining 19 ch (20 sts). Change to Tangerine yarn.
Row 2: Work into the front loop of the stitch only. 1 sc (dc) into each st of the previous row (20 sts). Change to Cyclamen yarn.
Row 3: 1 sc (dc) in each st of the previous row (20 sts). Change to Canary yarn.
Rows 4-14: Work Rows 2 to 12 of the instructions for age 0-3 months.
Fasten off.

6-9 months
Row 1 (bottom): Work 21 ch in Canary yarn. Work 1 sc (dc) in the 2nd ch from the hook, and 1 sc (dc) into each of the remaining 19 ch (20 sts). Change to Red yarn.
Row 2: 1 sc (dc) into each st of the previous row (20 sts). Change to Tangerine yarn.
Row 3: Work into the front loop of the stitch only. 1 sc (dc) into each st of the previous row (20 sts). Change to Cyclamen yarn.
Row 4: Sc (dc) into each st of the previous row (20 sts). Change to Canary yarn.
Rows 5-15: Work Rows 2 to 12 of the instructions for age 0-3 months.
Fasten off.

Place the front section onto the shoe with the last row at the toe, and use mattress stitch to sew the front part to the remaining 26/30/32 st of Rd 2. (Sew each st of Rd 2 of the shoe either to the end of a row of the front part or to a st in the last row.) Repeat for the second shoe.

WEDGE SANDALS

I want what Mummy's wearing! These chic shoes are perfect for the mini-me look. Without the heels for little ones, of course. .

MATERIALS

Crochet hook US B (2.5mm)
Schachenmayr original
Catania (50g/137yd/125m)
in Taupe (Col 254) and Light
Pink (Col 246), 50g each

HOW TO DO IT:

For one shoe

Work one sole in desired size in Taupe yarn, then continue in rounds as follows. Make sure that, with the exception of Rd 1 and 2 and the 1st rd in Light Pink yarn, you work alternately only into the back loop of the st, and then in the next st into the front loop of the st. This also applies when decreasing. In the WS rows, start with the other loop of the st, i.e. if you worked into the back loop of a st in a row, then work the first st into the front loop in the WS row, and vice versa.

Example: With 1 of the 2 st being worked tog, insert the hook into the back loop, and with the second one insert it into the front one.

Rd 1: 1 back post st (bp st) in each st of the previous rd (51/55/57 sts).
Rd 2: 1 front post st (fp st) into each st of the previous rd (51/55/57 sts). Fasten off.
Join the Light Pink yarn to the 37th/41st/43rd st of the previous rd. Continue working in rows. Work 1 ch at the end of each row and turn the work.

Row 1: Work into the back loop of the stitch only. 1 sc (dc) into each of the next 25 st (25 sts).
Rows 2–4: 1 sc (dc) into each st of the previous row (25 sts). Fasten off.
Join the yarn to the front loop of the 19th st of the last row. Work 1 ch and turn.
Row 5: Dec 1 st, 9 sc (dc), dec 1 st (11 sts). Do not work the remaining st.
Row 6: Dec 1 st, 7 sc (dc), dec 1 st (9 sts).
Rows 7 and 8: 1 sc (dc) into each st of the previous row (9 sts).
Row 9: Dec 1 st, 5 sc (dc), dec 1 st (7 sts).
Row 10: 1 sc (dc) into each st of the previous row (7 sts).
Row 11: *2 ch, 1 sl st*, rep from * to * 6 more times.
Fasten off.

TIES

Join the Light Pink yarn to the last st of Row 10 and crochet 51 ch, 1 sc (dc) into the 2nd ch from the hook, and 1 sc (dc) into each remaining ch. 1 sl st into Row 11. Fasten off.

Join the Light Pink yarn to the first sl st of the last st of Row 11 and crochet 51 ch, 1 sc (dc) into the 2nd ch from the hook, and 1 sc (dc) into each remaining ch. 1 sl st into Row 10.
Fasten off.

FRONT OF SHOE

Work in rows. Crochet 1 ch at the end of each row and turn the work. Crochet the front part of the shoe in the correct size in Light Pink following the instructions for the Espadrilles (page 60), without changing yarn colour. Make sure that you work alternately into the back loop of the

st only, and then in the next st into the front loop of the st. This also applies when decreasing.
Now place the front section onto the shoe with the last row at the toe, and use mattress stitch to sew the front part invisibly to the remaining 26/30/32 st of Rd 2. Sew each st o rd of the shoe either to the end of a row on the front section or to a st in the last row. Repeat for the second shoe.